NO ACCESS

BOSTON

NO ACCESS

BOSTON

BEANTOWN'S HIDDEN TREASURES, HAUNTS, AND FORGOTTEN PLACES

MARIA OLIA

Globe
Pequot

GUILFORD, CONNECTICUT

Globe
Pequot

An imprint of The Rowman & Littlefield Publishing Group, Inc.
4501 Forbes Blvd., Ste. 200
Lanham, MD 20706
www.rowman.com

Distributed by NATIONAL BOOK NETWORK

See photo credits on page 181

British Library Cataloguing in Publication Information available
Library of Congress Cataloging-in-Publication Data available

ISBN 978-1-4930-3593-9 (paperback)
ISBN 978-1-4930-3594-6 (e-book)

∞™ The paper used in this publication meets the minimum requirements of American
National Standard for Information Sciences—Permanence of Paper for Printed Library
Materials, ANSI/NISO Z39.48-1992

Printed in the United States of America

CONTENTS

INTRODUCTION

Where can you borrow life-size puppets? Why is there a marble staircase to nowhere in the atrium of the office building at Exchange Place? Where can you walk through a three-story glass globe as it existed in 1935? And what's with the vegetable farm on top of Fenway Park?

These are just some of the unusual, hidden, and little-known places that even life-long Bostonians may not know about. *No Access Boston: Beantown's Hidden Treasures, Haunts, and Forgotten Places* invites both the visitor and local to leave the beaten track, roam about, and explore some of the city's unknown and surprising places.

In its most literal sense, no-access travel is about exclusivity. In 1856 writer Oliver Wendell Holmes called Boston's State House, "the hub of the solar system." By extension, Bostonians consider the city "the hub of the universe." Hyperbole aside, there remain some places in the city such as the Harvard Club and the Boston Athenaeum that are generally not open to the public (Holmes, by the way, was both a Harvard man and a member of the Boston Athenaeum).

Other no-access sites are only for the most adventurous; so-called lost places such as Franklin Park Zoo's abandoned bear cages or Brook Farm, the forsaken home of Boston's nineteenth-century transcendentalist community.

Among this book's secret spots are the Japanese Garden behind the Museum of Fine Arts; the observation deck of the Custom House Tower; and Bodega, a sneaker boutique disguised as a Latino convenience market (a hidden door behind a vending machine slides open to reveal the store). Some of the places in *No Access Boston* require planning; only the National Park Service offers tours to Boston Light—by ferry and either once or twice a day on summer weekends. And if you want to see the crypt and belfry at Old North Church their "behind-the-scenes" tour is the one to book. Finally, there is a whole category of places that require readers to look more closely at the urban landscape around them; places like the bronze Salada Tea Doors in the Back Bay or the Fenway Victory Gardens, that people pass every day without noticing.

Whether it's your first time in Boston or you are back for more, *No Access Boston* will help you learn something new about the city.

ACORN STREET ON BEACON HILL

ENDEARINGLY QUAINT

With its seasonal window boxes, flickering gas lamps, and cobble-stones, Acorn Street is always camera-ready.

Discreet signs warn: "Private Street No Parking No Stopping and Dangerous Pass-ing," but that doesn't stop hordes of cell phone–toting travelers looking for the perfect Boston shot for their Instagram feeds.

Acorn Street, barely ten feet wide, was originally the servants' alley between the chic Federal brick townhomes that still stand on Mount Vernon and Chestnut Street. It was the place where the garbage was dumped, the privies stood, and the laundry was hung. Suzanne Besser is a Beacon Hill resident and former Executive Director of the Beacon Hill Civic Association. "Acorn Street was also called the kitchen street. Today there are nine individual houses on Acorn Street—and they are small by Beacon Hill standards—generally there are two rooms on each of four floors. It's vertical living."

The hilly peninsula along where Colonial Boston was first founded was known as Shawmut by the Massachusetts, the Native American tribe of the region. In 1630, when the Puritans sailed into what is now Boston Harbor, they established one of their first settlements near a fresh water spring in the area of present-day Beacon Hill.

This area was originally known as Trimount because of the three contiguous peaks: Cotton Hill, West Hill, and Sentry Hill that dominated the landscape. Sentry Hill was the tallest peak and became the site of a warning beacon. From 1635 to 1789 a succession of

beacon towers were built (some were blown away by the weather) and the neighborhood became known as Beacon Hill.

In 1795 the building of the new Massachusetts State House by Charles Bulfinch, the leading American architect of the time, paved the way for residential development of the neighborhood. By the early 1800s, Cotton Hill and West Hill were shorn off—the material was used as landfill as Boston made itself bigger and Beacon Hill became flatter and easier to build upon.

Even as it came to be, Beacon Hill was one of Boston's most expensive and exclusive neighborhoods—"where the Lowells speak only to the Cabots and the Cabots speak only to God"—and it remains so today. Former Secretary of State John Kerry and his wife Teresa Heinz are perhaps the most notable current residents, but over the years dozens of authors have called Beacon Hill home, including Louisa May Alcott, Robert Frost, and Sylvia Plath. Until 2016, historian David McCullough lived here as well.

Today all Beacon Hill businesses and residences must abide by the rules of the very preservation-minded Beacon Hill Civic Association. Surprisingly, the neighborhood window box decorations are not coordinated—they all just happen to look gorgeous year-round.

Besser lived on Acorn Street for five years before moving around the corner on West Cedar Street. "Most of the tourists on Acorn Street are very interested in Boston history. And they would always say the most complimentary things about the houses. It gives you a certain pride in where you live."

And while strolling Acorn Street is both undeniably romantic and a history-lover's delight, these cobbles are large and uneven so leave the heels behind and wear either comfortable flats or sneakers.

AFTERNOON TEA AT THE BOSTON PUBLIC LIBRARY

AN AFTERNOON TEA AT THE LIBRARY THAT IS WORTH CHECKING OUT

There is nothing quite like the calming peace and pleasure of a library. And while Boston's riotous colonialists may have had their trouble with tea, afternoon tea still has its loyalists in the city. As it turns out, afternoon tea and a library are a delightful combination.

When it opened in 1895, the Boston Public Library was praised as a "palace of the people." The Beaux Arts building, designed by Charles Follen McKim, anchors the Dartmouth and Boylston corner of Copley Square. Established in 1852, the Boston Public library is the country's oldest free municipal public library and it is the second largest library in the United States, outranked only by the Library of Congress. David Leonard is the library's president. "The Boston Public Library is loved. It is iconic. It's a treasure which periodically requires us to make sure that the building remains in pristine condition."

Both historic and cutting edge—the library completed an extensive $78 million renovation in 2016—the Boston Public library continues to be one of the city's most inviting public spaces. The required stop for visitors? The Bates Hall Reading Room is nothing short of breathtaking with its barrel vaulted coffered ceiling, time-worn oak tables, and emerald-green-glass reading lamps. Leonard says it is one of the most photographed spaces in Boston.

Ginger Lemon

The pungency of ginger is accented with lemon note, blended with the honey sweetness of linden

The Boston Public Library is filled with a priceless collection of volumes and artifacts. Among its holdings are a Shakespeare First Folio and an outstanding collection of Boston and New England maps—some date from as early as the seventeenth century. Among the Boston Public Library's art treasures are a series of murals, *The Triumph of Religion* by John Singer Sargent, and a set of bronze doors by Daniel Chester French. Free art and architecture tours are offered once a day—check the library's website for times.

Afternoon tea is among the most civilized of meals. Celebrating afternoon tea at the Boston Public Library offers visitors both bookish inspiration and an opportunity to reflect and refresh.

The library's afternoon tea takes place Tuesday through Sunday at the first floor Courtyard Restaurant, a space that was once the library's carriage house and stables. The handsome room is decorated in soft plum and grey and is drenched in sunlight from the floor-to-ceiling windows that overlook the library's lush Italianate courtyard. It's easy to forget you are in the heart of downtown Boston.

After being shown to a table, visitors are handed vintage books with the seasonal set menu tucked inside. Choose from a wide selection of regional English tea, rare blends, and herbal infusions. Or up the ante with a glass of bubbly.

This is a reassuredly traditional tea with fine bone china, starched white linen, and a three-tier cake stand that overflows with delights. The top plate is made up of both plain and currant scones accompanied by lemon curd, clotted cream, and marmalade. But do start with the bottom tier of savories. There are the expected English tea sandwiches, such as cucumber, salmon, and chicken salad, but that isn't all. There are also always a few creative offerings such as a delicate roasted Portobello mushroom and goat cheese crostini or lobster salad on a mini brioche (this is New England after all). Pretty cakes and pastries adorn the middle tier, which includes a tea-infused shortbread, fruited spice cake, decadent chocolate mini-cake triangles, pastel colored macarons, and a petite lemon meringue tart. It is best to pace yourself.

St. Paul   St. Matthew   St. Mark   St. Andrew   Sacred Heart of Jesus   Our Lady of Grace   St. Luke   St. John   St. Philip   St. S

INEXHAUSTIBLE FOUNTAIN OF MERCY   LADY OF THE MIRACULOUS MEDAL

e Pio   St. Lucy   St. Anthony of Padua   St. Michael   The Infant of Prague   Our Lady of Mercy   St. Raphael   St. Joseph   St. Martha   St. Jude Thaddeus   St. Therese of Lisieu

ninic   St. Thomas Aquinas   St. Martin de Porres   St. Catherine   St. Francis   The Divine Mercy   Lady of Guadalupe   St. Elizabeth   St. Raymond   St. Peregrine   St. Vincent de Paul   St. Jc

JESUS, I TRUST IN YOU   PATRON OF THE AMERICAS

Monica   Blessed Kateri Tekakwitha   St. Alphonsus Liguori   St. Gerard   St. John Neumann   Blessed Virgin Mary   The Divine Child   St. Patrick   St. Barbara   St. Benedict   St. Dyr

Symbol of the innocence of faith

St. Christopher   St. Cecilia   St. Agatha   St. Nicholas   Virgin of San Juan de los Lagos   Niño De Atocha   St. Florian   St. Maximilian Kolbe   St. Anne   St. George

ALL SAINTS WAY

ONE MAN'S PERSONAL PIETY
ON PROUD DISPLAY

In Boston's North End swarms of tourists walk down Hanover Street daily, following the path of the Freedom Trail past the Paul Revere House and Old North Church. This is also Boston's beloved Italian-American enclave, the home of dozens of restaurants and pastry shops.

The Big Dig brought down the Central Artery, making the North End much more accessible to development—as well as rising rents and gentrification. But this is still a neighborhood defined by both charm and tradition—and it even has a few remaining Italians.

Most Saturday mornings, life-long North End resident Peter Baldassari greets visitors in front of the door of a small alley located at the intersection of Hanover and Battery Streets. Every inch of wall space between the two red brick walk-up apartment buildings is filled with newspaper clippings, art pieces, and figurines of Catholic saints. The informal shrine is Baldassari's personal passion; he began collecting saint prayer cards when he was a school boy nearly seventy years ago. In the early 1990s he created All Saints Way.

Baldassari points out a few of his favorites: Mother Cabrini, the first American saint; Saint Rocco, the patron saint of sickness and pestilence; and Saint Patrick, beloved by Boston's Irish community. Baldassari loves sharing his knowledge of the saints with

visitors, "Did you know that Saint Anthony was born in Portugal? That his father was a governor? People think he was Italian. He wasn't Italian. There you go."

All Saints Way is certainly one of the city's quirkiest sites and Baldassari is one of the North End's true characters. He is open when he can and some nights he can have as many as a hundred visitors. He also accepts donations. "This is my stuff. People love it. This is part of Boston. It is part of me."

BEAR CAGE HILL

A ZOO FORGOTTEN BY TIME

Tucked in a quiet corner of Boston's Franklin Park, sit century-old bear dens that were abandoned and left to rot for decades. Today the crumbling historic structures, with their rusty iron work, knee-high weeds, and graffiti, have become a hotspot for urban explorers.

These woods might have been reclaimed by Mother Nature long ago—except that Franklin Park is hallowed ground for Boston's high school and college cross-country community and pounding feet have eroded much of the terrain's undergrowth. Bear Cage Hill is well-known as a steep, ankle-twisting feature on the Franklin Park cross-country course, which is legendary for its difficulty as much as for its rugged beauty.

Built in 1912, the bear exhibit was designed in an open-air grotto style with large boulders, native trees, and a fresh water pool. The first bears roamed freely within the enclosure—which was considered cutting edge for the time.

At 527 acres, Franklin Park is the city's largest park, and is considered the "crown jewel" of Boston's Emerald Necklace, named in honor of Benjamin Franklin (who made his name in Philadelphia, but was born and raised in Boston). The zoo's original plan was designed in 1885 by Frederick Law Olmsted in the pastoral picturesque style for which he was known. Olmsted died in 1903 and never saw the completion of his plans for Franklin Park. Soon after, in order to bolster attendance to the park, Olmsted's plans were altered to include a modest zoo of native animals in a naturalistic setting that was free to all.

Over the years, Franklin Park Zoo expanded, and throngs came to visit—with as many as two million visitors in 1920. However, The Great Depression and World War II marked a trying time for the zoo. With Bostonians going hungry, the city was faced with the challenge of spending its limited resources to feed and care for the animals. By the 1950s, they began charging zoo admission, but with tight times the exhibits had deteriorated and the animal population dwindled. Franklin Park's bear dens were eventually closed in 1970.

Today's Franklin Park Zoo comprises seventy-two acres and includes a popular children's barnyard and Tropical Forest exhibit. In 1997 management of the zoo was assumed by the non-profit Zoo New England, paving the way for a period of expansion that continues today.

To access Bear Cage Hill, walk across the small parking lot at the giraffe entrance (Pierpont Road) of Franklin Park Zoo and follow the small walking trail through the area known as Long Crouch Woods. You will reach a clearing and a wide stone staircase, which leads to the bear dens and a view of the city skyline. There is a posted "No Trespassing" sign. It is a sensible warning—this is not a place to visit alone or at night.

BEHIND THE SCENES TOUR OF SYMPHONY HALL

ACOUSTICS THAT ARE PITCH PERFECT

Boston's Symphony Hall is home to the celebrated orchestra that bears its name. Symphony Hall symbolizes pride of cultural place for many Bostonians. The Boston Symphony has always been part of the city's intellectual life and generations of New England families have made a December outing to Boston to see a Holiday Pops concert a Christmas tradition.

There's a magical quality to concerts at Symphony Hall—there is an intimacy between the orchestra and the audience that, along with excellent acoustics, makes this one of the world's best classical concert halls. When attending a Symphony Hall concert, book a backstage tour to fully appreciate this architectural gem. Free public tours are offered from October through May (check the website for days and times), and start at the stage door on St. Stephens Street.

The Boston Symphony was founded in 1881 by Major Henry Lee Higginson, a Civil War hero, banker, and amateur musician. Wendy Laurich, a long-time member of the Boston Symphony Association of Volunteers and an engaging tour guide, stops in front of a large portrait of Higginson that hangs in the BSO lobby and says, "We wouldn't have anything if it weren't for this one man."

By the late 1800s the BSO had outgrown its first home, the Boston Music Hall, which was located on Washington Street (it exists today as the Orpheum Theater).

In the decades after the Civil War, Boston's development steadily moved westward to the tidal marsh along the Charles River. In 1892, shortly after the land was filled, Higginson bought a parcel of land in Boston's Fenway neighborhood to construct a new concert hall. The architect of the Boston Public Library at Copley Square, Charles Follen McKim, was chosen to design it.

Ground was broken for the building in October 1899, and the hall was ready for its inaugural concert a year later. Compared to some of Europe's great concert halls that were also built around the same time, such as Vienna's Musikverein and Amsterdam's

Concertgebouw, Symphony Hall is a little plain. Says Laurich, "They didn't have a whole lot of money, but it was enough. Symphony Hall cost half a million dollars to build, but in those days, it was a fortune."

The Renaissance Revival building's façade lacks ornament, featuring red brick and limestone trim. The building also seems oddly sited—the broad granite steps and colonnaded portico on Huntington Avenue mark the building's original entrance. In the 1940s an underpass built along Huntington Avenue forced the BSO to shift the main entrance to what was the carriage entrance on Massachusetts Avenue—and it is the building's main entrance today.

The lobby stairs feature an elaborate wrought iron railing with a repeated "BMH" motif. When the stairs were cast it was thought the building would be named the Boston Music Hall. Even when it was decided to name the building Symphony Hall, they still installed the "BMH" iron railings—old money Bostonians were (and still are) thrifty.

Symphony Hall is a relatively small hall that seats 2,600 patrons. The ornate gold proscenium at the front of the stage is certainly one of the hall's focal points. At its top, Beethoven's name stands alone, while the eight medallions along the sides of the arch are empty. As Laurich explains, "The others

are blank because no one could agree on which other composers should be there."

Even by today's standards, Symphony Hall's shoe-box-shaped concert hall has remarkable acoustics and has influenced several concert halls around the world. Because of the groundbreaking work of Wallace Sabine, a young Harvard physics professor, Symphony Hall is one of the first concert halls designed according to scientific formulas.

The basement level of the hall is its working heart that buzzes with activity on concert days. The walkways are littered with the massive cargo boxes used to fly the musicians' instruments when the orchestra goes on tour. There are several sound-proof practice rooms that are used by the musicians either for themselves or as studio space for tutoring the next generation of orchestra players. In the back, there's a large workshop for the staff who keep the hall clean and running. There's also a newly renovated in-house recording room where the Boston Symphony mixes and masters their own recordings under the Deutsche Gramophon label. The BSO also records nearly every concert that takes place at Symphony Hall. Laurich says that conductor Andris Nelsons often comes down to the recording room right after a concert to analyze the evening's performance.

A service elevator brings tour-goers to the stage level where there are dressing rooms for the musicians and three green rooms—one for the conductor and two for musical guests or soloists. Visitors are ushered by vintage wooden musicians' lockers to the tuning room, where the musicians hang out. During intermission, it's "a hustle and a bustle," according to Laurich. Tour visitors are generally not allowed to walk on stage, but visitors do go backstage where there are monitors with a live-video feed of the hall. The backstage doors have little peepholes at various heights—and those are still used by the musicians and stage crew. Tours end with a demonstration of the magnificent 5,000-pipe 1947 Aeolian Skinner organ—and Symphony Hall rumbles.

BLACK HERITAGE TRAIL

UNCOVERING THE HISTORY
OF THE ABOLITIONIST MOVEMENT
IN BOSTON

You've heard about the Freedom Trail. But do you know about Boston's Black Heritage Trail? Walk through the small streets and alleys of Boston's Beacon Hill neighborhood to learn about prominent members of Boston's early black community and the critical role they played in ending slavery in the United States.

Boston's black community has a long history. The first African people arrived by slave ship in 1638. By the early 1700s there was a large community of both enslaved and free blacks in the North End. By the late 1700s, much of the community migrated to the north slope of Beacon Hill.

Boston's Black Heritage Trail starts near the end of the story, at the Robert Gould Shaw Memorial on the Boston Common, directly across the street from the State House. The striking bronze relief sculpture is a moving tribute to the 54th Massachusetts Regiment, the first volunteer black unit to fight in the Civil War.

Established in 1863 as a black regiment, the 54th was not allowed to have black officers. Robert Gould Shaw, raised in Boston and the son of abolitionist parents, was recruited to train and lead what was considered at the time to be a great experiment. The monument depicts the men marching down Beacon Street toward the ships that would take them to South Carolina where Shaw and many of his men would lose

their lives at Fort Wagner—if the story is familiar, perhaps it is because the battle was depicted in the movie *Glory*.

The Shaw Memorial took fourteen years to complete and is considered the masterwork of Augustus St. Gaudens. Shaw is shown on his horse marching alongside his men. The soldiers' faces are brave and determined—very different from the racialized stereotypes of African-Americans during the Civil War era.

Although slavery was abolished in Massachusetts in 1783, and Boston was seen as a center of the antislavery movement in the decades leading up to the Civil War, slavery was integral to the region's economy. The Brahmin families who lived on the south slope of Beacon Hill, such as the Lowells and Lawrences, may not have directly owned enslaved people but they were complicit in the institution of slavery by buying raw cotton in the South, transporting it to their factories and mills, and turning the cotton into finished goods that could be sold for a high profit. As Charles Sumner, a prominent Bay State abolitionist put it, "There is an unholy alliance between the lords of the lash and the lords of the loom."

Many of the houses in the neighborhood are registered Underground Railroad sites. The Black Heritage trail winds in and out of the narrow streets and alleys that

honeycomb Beacon Hill. A fugitive slave could cut through these streets with its many front doors and back doors. Places like Holmes Alley protected slaves from kidnappers and slave catchers.

Among the stops on the trail is the 1797 home of Black Revolutionary War hero George Middleton. As Chris Robinson, a National Park Service Ranger and guide says, "How often do we talk about black Revolutionary soldiers? Never, but they absolutely existed." Middleton led an all-black militia unit known as the Bucks of America, which served as the home guard for the city during the Siege of Boston. After the Revolutionary War, Governor John Hancock presented the unit with its own regimental flag—it is on display in the State House today.

Free guided walking tours of the Black Heritage Trail are given by well-informed National Park Service rangers throughout the year. Check the NPS website for dates and times or pick up a trail map at Faneuil Hall or Boston's Museum of African American History.

The tour ends at Smith Court and the African Meeting House that dates from 1806 and is the country's oldest extant black church building. Today authors and historians give talks about their latest books and research. Next door is the Abiel Smith School, founded in 1835 as the country's first public school for black children. Today the school is the site of Boston's Museum of African American History. So, after more than two hundred years, the original functions of a church and school as gathering places for educating the public about Boston's black community are still very much in use.

BODEGA

A SNEAKER STORE BEHIND A STORE

One of the biggest and best luxury streetwear retailers in the world just so happens to be located in Boston. The store is definitely a hidden gem. It is so off the beaten path that you have to know what you are looking for to find it.

Customers enter through what appears to be a bodega, a Latino corner store selling things like milk, eggs, beans, laundry detergent, and cat litter. But it's what lies behind that you will want to explore. Walk through to the back of the store and find

the Snapple vending machine. Wait and the door will slide open to reveal a modern showroom that features back-lit clothing displays, minimalist glass cases, and super-organized rows of hard-to-find sneakers like special edition Vans and the latest kicks by Rick Owens for Adidas.

It feels like a store you would find in New York or Los Angeles. Founded by partners Oliver Mak, Jay Gordon, and Dan Natola in 2006, Bodega is a veteran of the world streetwear scene. Says Mak, "We all met through organizing events around the intersection of art, fashion, and design. That was in the early 2000s."

As for the store's concept, Mak and his partners approached the store's design as installation art. "We were focused on the experience of hunting for non-mass prod-ucts that were rooted in counter culture and curated from around the world."

The store is a must-visit among Boston's homegrown clothing shops. Mak explains, "Any time anyone is in town who is inter-ested in our level of fashion, they make their way to us." Bodega has expanded over the years with an online presence since 2012. In early 2018 Bodega debuted a boutique in Los Angeles. "Even though Bodega is a trusted brand and has been in the industry for years," says Mak, "there are people find-ing us every day."

THE BOSTON ATHENAEUM

SECRETS INSIDE: WASHINGTON'S LIBRARY AND A BOOK BOUND IN HUMAN SKIN

Before there were public libraries, people paid for the privilege of borrowing books. Across the street from the State House is an exclusive library that even after more than two hundred years is unknown to most Bostonians.

Founded in 1807, The Boston Athenaeum is one of the oldest private lending libraries in America. It's a glorious space, housed in an 1849 Renaissance Revival building filled with stacks and stacks of books, original art work, antique rugs, long wooden reading tables, and cozy nooks in quiet corners. It's a place that commands reverence.

There is something magical about its fractional street address and red leather doors, but, unlike most libraries, you have to pay to use it. Non-members can pay an admission fee to utilize the library on a per-visit basis. The public is also welcome to many of the athenaeum's lectures. Another way to visit? Public art and architecture tours are offered several times a week to non-members for a small fee.

Athenaeums are a library/museum hybrid; a social library that also serves as a temple of learning. It's a place that celebrates books with author talks and discussion groups. A recent topic was "People Before Highways: Boston Activists, Urban Planners and a New Movement for City Making." The athenaeum also hosts small concerts and wine social hours.

The Gordon Newspaper Room may be known as the "napping room" by longtime members, but lately the athenaeum has been rediscovered by young creatives looking

for quiet co-working space. Membership at the athenaeum has increased 74 percent over the past five years and now there are about forty-five hundred active members.

There is a wide array of art work to discover very up close and personal; pieces by John Singer Sargent, Gilbert Stuart, and Augustus Saint Gaudens. Among the athenaeum's treasures are books from George Washington's personal library as well as the King Chapel Collection—dating from 1698, it is the oldest surviving Colonial library in Boston. Among the athenaeum's more astonishing items is a book bound in human skin.

The Boston Athenaeum is a must-visit for the literary minded. And while the air of antiquity may be intimidating, don't be fooled—it really is open to all.

BOSTON HARBOR ISLANDS

IS THERE ANYTHING MORE
"NO ACCESS" THAN AN ISLAND?

Not that long ago, Boston was known nationally for its dirty water. As recently as the 1980s Boston Harbor reeked of sewage and trash. Today, after a court-ordered cleanup, the harbor dazzles.

Just a short ferry ride from downtown Boston are some of the city's greatest treasures—the Boston Harbor Islands. Considered an archipelago, these fifteen hundred acres of land (at low tide; at high tide the acreage is closer to three thousand acres) that make up the Boston Harbor Islands National and State Park encompass some thirty-four islands and peninsulas within a twelve-mile radius of the city.

There are large islands such as Peddocks with its marina, sandy beaches, and hiking trails and tiny outcroppings such as Nix's Mate, which in the 1700s was the location of the gallows where pirates were hung and displayed for all ships to see as they sailed in and out of Boston Harbor.

Six of the islands—Georges, Spectacle, Peddocks, Lovells, Bumpkin, and Grape are publically accessible by ferry from Boston. Georges and Spectacle are the most popular for visitors with a mix of recreational activities, including a Civil War fort, drumlins to hike, and opportunities to camp and swim.

Georges Island acts as the gateway to all the islands with a large visitor's center, a snack bar, and a small museum. The mighty star-shaped granite citadel that nearly fills the island is Fort Warren. Constructed from 1833 through 1860, it was once a POW camp for

some two thousand Confederate soldiers. Fort Warren was also strategically important for the protection of Boston Harbor and remained active during the Spanish American War, World War I, and World War II.

During the two World Wars, the Charlestown Navy Yard, the Fore River Shipyard in Quincy, and the Hingham Shipyard turned out thousands of destroyers and cargo ships for the US Navy. Those ships first entered the Atlantic at Boston Harbor and Fort Warren's cannons (although never tested) protected the harbor's main shipping channels.

To wander the island on your own, walk across the drawbridge and pass through the oak and iron sallyport to the expansive parade grounds. Explore the dark tunnels and passageways of the prisoners' quarters. Take a stroll high along the sod-covered ramparts and look down across the harbor and see Little Brewster Island and Boston Light, the nation's oldest lighthouse station, dating from 1716.

National Park Rangers give frequent tours of the fort. Just be on the lookout for the Lady in Black. Legend has it that Mrs. Andrew Lanier, the wife of a Confederate soldier, wanders the grounds of Fort Warren in her black robes after being hanged for trying to help her prisoner husband escape.

Just a fifteen-minute ferry ride from Boston, Spectacle Island is the closest harbor island to the city. Early explorers named it Spectacle Island because the two tall bluffs on either end are connected by a sand bar and resemble a pair of glasses.

Over the years Spectacle Island has had many uses. It was pasture land, the site of a small pox quarantine facility, a horse-rendering factory, and an illegal gambling den. Until the 1950s, it was one of the city's dumps (the trash would sometimes combust spontaneously). The $12 billion Big Dig/Central Artery project was one of the largest highway construction projects in the United States—and six million tons of excavated dirt were shipped over to Spectacle Island to seal the landfill.

These days Spectacle Island is home to a life-guarded beach and a snack bar (that closes when the food runs out by late afternoon). There are also five miles of grassy walking trails with an abundance of thistle and wild beach roses that lead to hills forested with pine and oaks that look out to views of the Boston skyline.

BOSTON HARBOR LIGHTHOUSE TOUR

BOSTON LIGHT: AMERICA'S FIRST LIGHTHOUSE STATION

Solitary, sturdy sentinels of the New England coast, lighthouses are among the region's most iconic images. Boston still has three historic lighthouses that guide the way for ships into Boston Harbor, their beams of light sweeping the water up to twenty-seven miles out to sea.

Boston's Harbor's lighthouses are remote—each is located on an island or rock outcropping in the middle of the Atlantic. But although Boston Harbor's lighthouses are challenging to visit, the National Park Service does allow the general public access, including boat transportation.

Boston Lighthouse Cruises by the National Park Service take place from June through September, generally on Saturday as well as some Fridays and Sundays. There are only one or two departures per day and seating is limited, so reservations in advance are a necessity.

The three-and-a-half-hour cruise tours are fully narrated by National Park Service Rangers who are experts about the history of Boston Harbor. US Coast Guard volunteers are also on hand to offer insights into lighthouse keepers' isolated lives. Says Coastguard Auxiliary Assistant Keeper Audrey Tessier, "On days when we are totally socked in, you can feel like you are the only person there."

Bonus sights on these voyages include sunbathing harbor seals and large populations of water birds, including common terns, herons, and egrets.

The boat is well-equipped with a sun deck and a climate-controlled cabin to enjoy views of Long Island Head Light and Graves Light on the way to the voyage's highlight—an extended stop at Boston Light.

The boat first passes Long Island Head Light, which is the closest lighthouse to Boston. Its brick tower dates from 1900 and is just visible peeking out from heavy tree cover. The trip continues on to Graves Light, Boston Harbor's most remote lighthouse. The gray granite tower is located on a pile of treacherous rocks in the middle of the ocean and dates from 1905. The light has been privately owned since 2013 and is used as a vacation home, so it is not open to the public. However, the park boats will slowly circle the little island to allow lighthouse enthusiasts to take photos.

Finally the boat docks at Little Brewster Island with its lighthouse, a quaint keeper's house, a few outbuildings, and a stretch of shoreline. Erected in 1716, Boston Light has guarded the coastline and saved countless ships from wrecking along the treacherous outcroppings of rocky ledges in Boston's outer harbor. Although the first nine to fourteen feet of the tower is original, the rest dates from 1783, as the original lighthouse was blown up in 1776 when the British evacuated Boston.

Boston Light continues to be a major aid to navigation in the outer harbor as a light and fog signal station. Navigation technology has rendered lighthouses obsolete—there is no need for keepers to climb the stairs these days. But as Boston's first lighthouse, Boston Light has the distinction of being the country's only Coast Guard lighthouse with a resident keeper.

Tessier says that every one of Boston Light's seventy keepers has a special story. She tells the tale of Boston Lighthouse's first keeper, George Worthylake, who grew up on nearby George's Island. In 1718, soon after taking the job of lighthouse keeper, Worthylake drowned, along with a slave, his wife, and young daughter when their rowboat capsized while returning from Boston.

"It's a fascinating story, but unfortunately a tragic one."

The current keeper of Boston Light is Sally Snowman and she is Boston Light's first woman keeper. Snowman has tended Boston Light since 2003, and she's as much a historian as she is a caretaker. On tour days, she comes out to greet visitors wearing a bonnet and a dress based on what a seventeenth-century fisherman's wife might wear. Visitors have the opportunity to climb the lighthouse's seventy-six spiraling steps into the lamp room to watch the Fresnel lens rotate. This is also a great place from which to take in skyline views of Boston ten miles away. As Tessier says, "Spending time out at Boston Light puts in perspective the importance of things. How big you are in comparison. The island has its own rhythms. It's rejuvenating."

BRATTLE BOOK SHOP

A COZY LITTLE BOOK SHOP FULL OF RARE AND WONDERFUL GEMS

This one-of-a kind bookstore offers bibliophiles much more than a well-curated selection of books, packing an abundance of quirky charm and Boston history within its walls.

The original Brattle Book Shop was founded in 1825 in Cornill, the bookish heart of nineteenth-century Boston, which was home to many of the city's publishing companies. The shop has been owned by the Gloss family since 1949 and moved to its current location in 1984. Current proprietor Ken Gloss is a bit of a local celebrity; he is a regular appraiser on PBS's *Antique Roadshow*. "Not many cities have a place like the Brattle Book Shop," says Gloss. "I think that it's one of the places that makes Boston unique."

A mix of new, used, and out-of-print classics dominate the shelves on the first and second floors. But if you're looking for an ideal gift for a special occasion, the third-floor is where it's at. Here, the rare book room holds the store's real treasures like first editions and signed copies as well as second-hand antiquarian titles like *Mrs. Frazier's Practice of Cookery, Pastry and Confectionary*, printed around 1806 in Edinburgh, or a signed copy of *Transformations* by Anne Sexton.

"There have been a lot of interesting buys," says Gloss. "It's a treasure hunt. More recently I appraised a book for a woman on Martha's Vineyard. It was a biography of Jackie Robinson. Nothing special. It would normally sell for ten dollars. It was inscribed to her mother, 'Thank you for letting me stay with you for a year when I came to New

$5 Each 🍎

Books with
Yellow Sticker

Please Pay Inside

OK ROOM

FROM OUR THIRD

FROM OUR THIRD FLOOR RARE BOOK ROOM

FROM OUR RARE BOOK ROOM

From Our Third Floor Rare Book Roo

OR RARE BOOK ROOM

FROM OUR RARE BOOK ROOM

FROM OUR THIRD FLOOR RARE BOOK R

The Author's Edition de Luxe of Mark Twain's Works is limited to 620 copies, of which only 600 copies are for sale in Great Britain and its Dependencies.

This is No. 524.

S.L. Clemens (Mark Twain)

Signed Mark Twain Author's Edition de Luxe 25 volumes
$8,500

NATIONAL GAME

A. G. SPALDING

A.G. Spalding's America's National Game, inscribed to teammate and early Hall-of-Famer
George Wright (both pictured); with additional annotations by Wright...$12,500

THE WRITINGS OF HENRY DAVID THOREAU

A WEEK ON THE CONCORD AND MERRIMACK RIVERS

BOSTON AND NEW YORK
HOUGHTON MIFFLIN AND COMPANY
MDCCCCVI

The Writings of Thoreau, 1906
Manuscript Edition, in 20 volumes
$8,750

SOLD

Audubon's Birds 1840-44 $35,000

SOLD

A. Lincoln.

Signed Photograph of Abraham Lincoln

Frederick Douglass' Paper.

VOL. VI.—NO. 18.

FREDERICK DOUGLASS' PAPER is
PUBLISHED AT BUFFALO STREET (OPPOSITE THE
ARCADE) BY FREDERICK DOUGLASS.

TERMS:

74 Issues of Douglass'
anti-slavery newspaper

National Park
aho, Nevada, Colorado, and Utah
Thomas Moran, 1876
00

York.' Robinson stayed with the family when he first signed with the Dodgers because no one would rent to a black man at that time."

The shop has always had a serious following among students, downtown office workers, and Boston's literati. In recent years it has become a big destination for tourists.

The open-air bookstore in the empty lot next door features used books and has always attracted casual browsers looking for a bargain—prices are just three or five dollars. The Brattle Book Shop sale lot has also become well known as one of Boston's most photogenic spots, no filter necessary. Says Gloss, "There was a recent list of cliché photos in Boston, and we made near the top of the list. We love being a cliché."

BROOK FARM

OF THIS UTOPIA,
THERE IS HARDLY A TRACE

Visitors to Brook Farm will need to do some historical detective work. Located in the neighborhood now known as West Roxbury, the secular Utopian farming community was greatly influenced by the popular mid-nineteenth-century transcendental philosophy of self-reliance and social reform.

Few vestiges remain of the farm's original structures, only some remnants of foundations and long abandoned trails. It is a site where one might, with some imagination, picture the farm as it appeared in its heyday—an arresting scene of rolling meadows and a wooded forest bounded by a small brook and the Charles River.

Today it's not a bad bushwhack. Maggi Brown, a visitor supervisor at Massachusetts' Department of Conservation and Recreation, leads the way. "Much of the farm buildings were burned by vandals in the 1970s. These days, nature is having more impact on the farm than the public. We have invasive plants like bittersweet that reclaim the site quickly."

George Ripley and his wife Sophia Ripley, prominent Boston social reformers, founded the two-hundred-acre Brook Farm in 1841, which at its peak numbered 120 participants. Members farmed the land and were encouraged to pursue self-realization through the study of nature, science, literary pursuits, and the arts. However, most in the community were intellectuals and had no experience farming. Brown says, "What

they didn't realize was that being a farmer in New England wasn't easy at all. Brook Farm was a dismal economic failure."

Rooted in the ideals of transcendentalism, a golden age of American literature was taking place in Boston at this time. Among transcendentalists' beliefs were that man himself could experience spiritual truths and that God was within the individual.

Authors Ralph Waldo Emerson, Nathaniel Hawthorne, and Margaret Fuller were prominent members of the movement. Emerson and Fuller were frequent visitors of Brook Farm; a young Hawthorne was a founding member and resident. At the beginning, Hawthorne thought the farm a lovely social experiment, saying he "felt the original Adam reviving in me." However, he was not keen on the manual labor required that left him little time for writing. He left the community after just six months and later wrote of the experience, "It is my opinion that a man's soul may be buried and perish under a dung-heap, or in a furrow field, just as well as under a pile of money."

It was a noble effort, but as is the case of most Utopian society attempts, the Brook Farm experiment was short-lived. From the beginning it was beset with money troubles and internal fighting. Ultimately a fire burned the principal residential building to the ground and the community disbanded

a military training site for Union soldiers during the Civil War. After the war the property was purchased by the Lutheran Church and converted to an orphanage. The Lutherans' print shop published bibles and pamphlets and is the only building that survived. Located close to the site's parking lot, the dilapidated structure is off-limits to visitors. A cemetery, the Gardens of Gethsemane, was established on part of the property in the 1870s and exists today. In 1988 the Brook Farm Historic Site was purchased by the state and is now open to the public. And although Brook Farm may be mostly gone, one may find a little bit of heaven on Earth rambling through its wild landscape.

in 1847, after a little more than six years in existence.

In 1861 the abandoned property was renamed Fort Andrew and was used as

HERE WERE RE-INTERRED

THE REMAINS OF PERSONS

FOUND UNDER THE BOYLSTON STREET MALL

DURING THE DIGGING OF THE SUBWAY

1895

CENTRAL BURYING GROUND

CENTURIES OF TALES TO TELL

Tucked away in the southeast corner of Boston Common sits a small unassuming Colonial-era cemetery. Within these iron gates and shaded by mature oak trees, rows of three-hundred-year-old slate headstones, weathered and worn, are arranged haphazardly.

Boston Common was founded in 1634, on the edge of what was then the Puritan settlement of Boston, as open pasture. It is considered the oldest public park in the country. Colonial Boston's population grew rapidly and establishing places to bury the dead was an early priority for the settlers.

As ancient as the Central Burying Ground is, it is actually the city's fourth cemetery with its first burials taking place in 1749. Regular interments in the Central Burying Ground ceased in the 1830s. In 1895, the country's first subway, the Tremont Street Subway, was constructed. Nearly a thousand nameless graves were discovered during the digging of the tunnels under the Boston Common. The remains were moved to a mass grave and a large simple head stone was erected in memoriam.

The Central Burying Ground is the final resting place of more than five thousand people from all walks of life, including colonists who participated in the Boston Tea Party or fought at the Battle of Bunker Hill, members of Boston's early Catholic (mostly French or Irish) community, and the unmarked graves of the city's desperately poor. During the Revolutionary War, the Boston Common became a staging area for the

British Army, so scores of British soldiers who died of either disease or combat during this time are buried here as well. The burying ground's most notable resident is artist Gilbert Stuart, who painted the most famed painting of George Washington (his unfinished portrait of Washington is the basis for the image that is on the US dollar bill).

Compared to the better-known Granary and Kings Chapel burying grounds on the other side of Boston Common, the Central Burying Ground maintains a peaceful and reverent atmosphere with plenty of space to meander and wander and imagine the landscape of Boston's Colonial past.

CUSTOM HOUSE TOWER

FOR ALTITUDE-LOVING TRAVELERS

There aren't a whole lot of buildings in Boston where you don't have to use an address when you get in a taxi, but the Custom House Tower is certainly one of them.

The sixteen-story Custom House Tower has been an elegant centerpiece of Boston's waterfront skyline since 1915 and is a cherished local landmark. Inspired by the Campanile at St. Mark's Basilica in Venice, the uppermost portion of the tower has marble and bronze clocks on each of its four sides and is topped by an elaborate triangular iron cap.

"Most people don't realize that the Custom House dials are the same size as Big Ben," says local clockmaker David Hochstrasser.

Located at the edge of the city's original shoreline and one of the first buildings visible to ships sailing into Boston Harbor, a Custom House has been located roughly on this same spot since the earliest days of Boston's settlement. In its heyday, the Custom House was a bustling place where brokers and custom agents worked together to build the wealth of a young nation. At one time the port of Boston accounted for one-fifth of all duties collected in the United States.

When it was finished in 1847, the Custom House was a monumental building for its time—and it was an example of an increased demand for better architectural standards for civic buildings. Architect Ammi B. Young was commissioned with the project—his

elaborate design featured a grand neoclassical building resembling a Greek temple with a massive portico held up by granite Corinthian columns and a skylit marble Roman rotunda.

But by the early 1900s, increased shipping into Boston meant still more space was needed. A slender 495-foot clock tower designed by the architectural firm of Peabody and Stearns was added to the existing two-story structure—making the Custom House Boston's first skyscraper. Remarkably, this was the city's tallest building until 1964 and the completion of the Prudential Center in the Back Bay. By the 1980s, Boston's US Custom Service operations had relocated to the Tip O'Neill Federal building around the corner at Government Center, and the Custom House was deemed "surplus" and sold to the city.

For much of the twentieth century, the Custom House clock was the central time piece in the Financial District. However, because of an undersized motor, the clock was famously inaccurate and was known as the "four-faced liar" by neighborhood office workers (sometimes late returning from their lunch break) because each side showed a slightly different time.

Throughout much of the 1980s the clock didn't run at all. Hochstrasser, along with his brother Ross, restored the clock in 1987—and has been keeper of the clock ever since. Still, unplanned stoppages are not uncommon. "If the wind blows long enough or hard enough, it will stop the clock. And it doesn't take much snow or ice on the hands to cause the clock to shut down altogether," said Hochstrasser. That the Custom House clock is still ticking despite its age and exposure to New England's weather is a testament to the Hochstrassers' care.

Winter brings its own challenges to the operation of the clocks, while spring brings some special visitors. By March falcons can be seen swooping in and out of the very top of the Custom House Tower. Various pairs of peregrine falcons have been raising their young at the Custom House since the 1980s—the nest is considered one of the most successful on the east coast. Endangered as recently as the 1960s, the peregrine falcon has made a comeback in recent decades. It is difficult to spot the nesting box on the thirtieth-floor ledge, but each batch of chicks has a worldwide audience thanks to a live streaming webcam that chronicles their growth.

Vacant for years, the building was leased in 1996 by Marriott International, which invested and reinvented the building to create Marriott Vacation Club Pulse at Custom House. Because of the building's landmark status, public access to the

Custom House was a condition of the property's development.

Today the Custom House is very much open to visitors—whether they stay at the hotel or not. Despite a lack of publicity, it's not unusual to see tourists wander into the lobby and poke around.

The building's original two floors are always open to the curious. From the white-marble-clad reception area, look up to see the Great Seal of the United States painted on the dome. Dating from 1960, this is the only painted Great Seal that exists in a non-federal building and the only seal not located

in Washington DC. Walk up the small staircase—it's not hard to imagine armed guards patrolling the iron cat walk above while watching taxes and duties being collected in the counting room below. The heraldic-like flags that hang from the rotunda represent the Boston merchant house families who made their fortunes in trade.

Of course, hotel guests have the best access of all and are able to go out on the observation deck at any time. Marriott offers its eighty-four Custom House rooms to non-vacation club-members. All the rooms are one-bedroom suites with a private bedroom and a separate living room with sleeper sofa. Families in particular love the rooms' layout. Hotel guests can also check out the mechanism that powers the clocks—it's located in the twenty-fourth-floor game room, right next to the pool table.

For all vista seekers, the open-air observation deck with its 360-degree view is the crown jewel of the building. There are never any crowds here, but access to the observation deck is unusually restricted, open to the public for only a short time each day. Non-hotel guests can meet in the lobby at 2 p.m. (Saturday through Thursday, weather permitting, call in advance, a small fee is charged) and a hotel worker will escort you to the twenty-sixth floor. Alternatively, buy a beverage at the Counting Room Bar (Saturday through Thursday, 6 to 7:30 p.m.) and head up to the deck and enjoy a drink with a view. Emerge from the elevator and outside onto the platform for a visceral experience: a dizzying panorama of the city in every direction as well as a powerful sense of the Custom House's dramatic architecture.

ETHER DOME

AN ARCHITECTURAL, HISTORIC, AND MEDICAL GEM

One of the city's more esoteric tourist offerings, the Ether Dome at Massachusetts General Hospital commemorates the 1846 discovery of ether's use as an anesthetic. Located deep within the hospital, this is a historic site for those prepared to make an effort. Mass General is a sprawling campus—check in at the information desk at the main entrance for in-hospital directions.

Boston's General Hospital, as it was first known, opened its doors in 1821. The hospital's original white granite building was designed by Charles Bulfinch in a neo-classical style with a pillared portico and crowned with a dome—Bulfinch's signature element.

Beneath the dome's skylight is the hospital's historic surgical amphitheater. It contains a stepped gallery of wooden benches that in the hospital's early days was used for students and observers to watch surgeons amputate limbs, remove tumors, and set broken bones. Without electricity or anesthesia, patients were lucky to have a sunny day for their operation—and a quick and skillful surgeon.

The discovery of ether's use as an anesthetic revolutionized surgery and changed medical history. On October 16, 1846, Dr. William Morton demonstrated the anesthetic effects of inhaled ether for a man undergoing a tumor removal before a group of physicians at Massachusetts General.

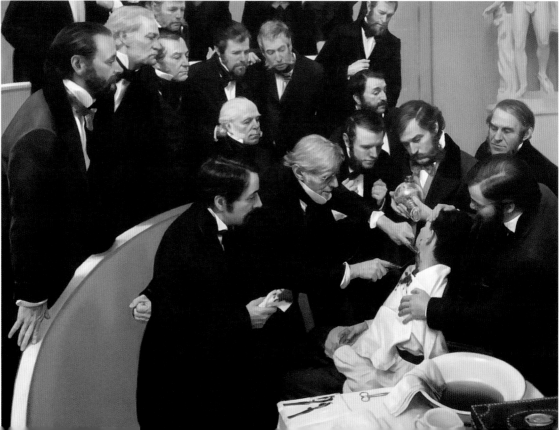

After exploring the room's unique architecture, investigate the quirky collection of medical artifacts, including cringe-inducing amputation saws and giant syringes dating from the nineteenth century.

Also here is Padihershef, a twenty-five-hundred-year-old Egyptian mummy that was a witness on the day that the milestone operation took place. "Padi," as he is affectionately called, was given to the city of Boston as a gift from a Dutch Merchant in 1823. One of the first Egyptian mummies to come to America, Padi, along with his painted inner and outer wooden coffins, was displayed on tour throughout the East Coast and marketed as a medical curiosity to fundraise for the hospital in its early years. Padi has resided in the operating theater since 1825 and is universally known as Mass General's oldest patient.

The Ether Dome is still a teaching amphitheater and is used for classes and seminars. The public is welcome to visit when the room is not in use to learn about a very interesting bit of Massachusetts medical history.

EXCHANGE PLACE STAIRCASE

A GOOD SAVE

Any building more than a hundred years old located in downtown Boston is bound to be historic. Located across the street from the Old State House, the 1896 Boston Stock Exchange Building was not only one of the country's oldest and largest office buildings, it was distinguished for another reason: the twelve-story brick and pink granite Italianate structure was an excellent example of Gilded Age opulence.

In the 1980s, the Boston Stock Exchange building was demolished, but the original State Street façade along with the ornate marble double staircase were saved from the wrecking ball. The historic State Street entrance is marked by the building's original bronze lanterns. The staircase was salvaged and stored during construction of the Exchange Place tower, and re-erected in the atrium lobby that unifies the two buildings.

The new forty-story glass and steel office tower rises next to its nineteenth-century counterpart, offering a stark juxtaposition between past and present.

This is one of downtown's high-profile office towers. *The Boston Globe* is one of the building's principal tenants—the newspaper moved here from its long-time Dorchester headquarters in 2017.

Lobby security is strict, but polite. The front desk security team is used to curiosity seekers looking at the staircase, but visitors are not to permitted to walk on the stairs (which lead to offices) or take photos. Use the Congress Street entrance for the best view of the staircase.

FENWAY FARMS

URBAN AGRICULTURE HITS
NEW HEIGHTS AT FENWAY PARK

Look up. If you can find this farm's fields, it is a pretty good guess you are in a ball park. Fenway Park. Literally.

Built in 1912, Fenway Park is America's oldest ballpark. In a 1960 *New Yorker* essay, Pulitzer prize–winning novelist John Updike famously observed, "Fenway Park, in Boston, is a lyric little bandbox of a ballpark." Even today, none of Boston's Red Sox fans, which is everybody, would disagree.

At the beginning of the 2015 baseball season, the Red Sox teamed up with Green City Growers, a Somerville-based commercial agriculture company to install an urban rooftop garden utilizing an underused parcel parallel to Fenway's third base line. Today, the five-thousand-square-foot Fenway Farms grows organic vegetables and herbs by the boxful and by the bushel—nearly six thousand pounds of produce annually—the majority of which is used at the EMC Club, the park's fine-dining restaurant, as well as at some of the stadium's concession stands.

Says Jessie Banhazi, Green City Grower's CEO and Founder, "It's our most visible project. We have exposure to half a million people a year who are learning about the farm through taking a Fenway Park tour or seeing a Red Sox game. It connects the Red Sox to the community while teaching fans where their food is coming from."

Fenway Farms is similar to many typical New England summer gardens, planted with lettuce, tomatoes, and zucchini. However, the Fenway Farm produce lineup also includes more unusual crops such as bok choy, pea shoots, fennel, and sweet potatoes.

"We work closely with the chefs at Fenway. They tell us what they want and we grow it for them," says Banhazi.

The production farm at Fenway features a sustainable design incorporating a recycled milk-crate growing system of raised beds that hold an organic blend of New England compost. The garden's watering needs are met with a state-of-the-art, weather-sensitive, drip irrigation system. As a rooftop garden, Fenway Farms has the benefit of full sun and also doesn't have the pesky pests—like ravaging rabbits and pillaging squirrels—that can be the bane of the home gardener.

It's hard not to be inspired by the sight of this thriving patch of green. And although fans do not have direct access to the Fenway Farms site, there are great views of the farm operation from the walkway along the State Street Pavilion level. There's always a lot of interest when the Green City Grower's team takes to their field to tend to the crops. In just a few seasons, Fenway Farms has already proven to be a hit with fans.

FENWAY VICTORY GARDENS

HELPING TO WIN THE WAR

People grow vegetables for food, to save money, and for exercise. But during World War II, vegetable gardening in America was considered patriotic—and could help save the world for democracy.

In World War II, America was fighting on two fronts and the government encouraged civilians to grow their own food to reduce pressure on the food supply. It is estimated that by 1944, 40 percent of all vegetables were grown from victory gardens across the United States.

Boston rose to the challenge admirably. The Boston Victory Garden Committee commandeered forty-nine plots for cultivation, including the Boston Common and the Boston Public Garden. A seven-acre parcel in the Fens, one of the six parklands that comprise Frederick Law Olmsted's "Emerald Necklace," became what is known as the Fenway Victory Gardens.

Hidden in plain sight—Fenway Park is so close to the gardens that you can hear the roar of the crowd on game days—Fenway Victory Gardens is one of only two surviving World War II victory gardens. With five hundred garden plots fully subscribed and an active waiting list, the Fenway Victory Gardens is as popular as ever.

This is a passionate group of community gardeners. Apart from the tidy vegetable plots and stunning flower beds, the Fenway Garden Society hosts dozens of workshops, such as "gardening for seniors" and "how to rabbit-proof your garden." The

society sponsors events as well, including community participation days and the very popular Open Gardens and Art Show.

"The Fenway Victory Garden is open for visitors, not just for gardeners," says Elizabeth Bertolozzi, the current president of the Fenway Garden Society. The public is always welcome to meander along the paths and peek over the fences.

Near the garden's entrance at Park Drive and Boylston Street, the gated Medicinal Herb Garden is the society's principal display garden and is always open to the public. It's an enchanting space with secluded benches and beds showcasing plants with healing properties, such as lavender, chamomile, and oregano.

Says Bertolozzi, "If people like to talk to gardeners, come on the weekends. That's a part of our mission, educating others on gardening techniques and involving the entire community."

STUDY for EL JALEO
by John S. Sargent

HARVARD ART MUSEUMS

BOOK A PRIVATE VIEWING
AT THE ART STUDY CENTER

For sheer jaw-dropping potential, few public art museums in the country rival the Harvard Art Museums. The museum is justly famous for its collection of American and European art, which is complemented by more than respectable holdings in Egyptian, Greek, Roman, Asian, and Near East art.

The museums' permanent collections include some 250,000 objects, but as is true with most art museums, just a tiny fraction, typically 5 percent or so, is on display at any one time for visitors to view and enjoy.

A $350 million renovation and expansion of the Harvard Art Museums was completed in 2014. Harvard's three art museums—the Fogg, the Busch-Reisinger, and Arthur M. Sackler—were united by a dazzling glass and steel roof design by museum maestro, Renzo Piano.

The entire fourth floor of the museum is dedicated to the Art Study Center. The rooms have a loft-like feel and are suffused with abundant natural light with lots of open table space along with walls for short-term display. Magnifying glasses make it easy for close examination of the art without the barriers normally needed for public display.

Harvard classes use the facility, as do neighboring universities. Scholars, artists, and curators across disciplines and from around the world engage in research at the

center, but the Art Study Center is available beyond the museum's immediate community. Says Janet Chen, one of the museum's art installers, "We have people who live in the neighborhood and just like to come in and look at art. It's a program for everybody."

It's an extraordinary opportunity to make the most of encounters with great works of art and experience the Harvard Art Museum collection in an exclusive way.

The program is free with museum admission, but it does involve a bit of anticipatory lead up—appointments should be reserved online at least two weeks in advance. Children must be over the age of fourteen and be accompanied by an adult. Visitors can use the Harvard Art Museum's online collection database to choose the works they wish to view.

Marvel at the workmanship of a 1762 silver porringer crafted by Paul Revere, browse through a curatorial box of nineteenth-century Boston streetscapes, or request a selection of the museum's many Andy Warhol works to compare and contrast. If it is safe to bring it out, the museum's art handlers will make it happen.

THE HARVARD CLUB OF BOSTON

HISTORY THROUGH THE KEYHOLE

Think private clubs with their leather wing chairs, wood paneling, and men with three last names are a relic of an earlier era? Think again. The Harvard Club of Boston—with upscale dining, a stunning four-story ballroom, and a well-appointed gym—is thriving. At today's Harvard Club, the city's old-guard establishment mixes with rising stars from the city's technology, life sciences, and healthcare sectors.

In the latter half of the nineteenth century, Boston's Brahmin elite founded several men-only private clubs. The Union and the Somerset are among the city's oldest and most durable institutions. They, along with the Harvard Club, have played a role in shaping Boston's business and social life, helping to transform what was a provincial capital into a sophisticated, world-class city.

Among its starchier neighbors, the Harvard Club has a reputation for diversity. It's clear from a display of headshots of the current Board of Governors that this is an old boys' club no more. Karen Galvin, the Harvard Club's head of marketing, says "People are always surprised to see how diverse our membership is. Of course, we are an alumni club, so we are as diverse as Harvard."

Boston's private clubs may seem secretive, even forbidding places to the casual passersby. Each of the city's private clubs is prominently located either on Beacon Hill or in the Back Bay, but you could walk by the entrance of any one of them dozens of times without realizing that they are there.

It was 1913 when the Harvard Club first opened its doors to the Back Bay Clubhouse on Commonwealth Avenue, which it still occupies today. In 1976 the Harvard Club Downtown Clubhouse, located in the heart of Boston's financial district, was established on the thirty-eighth floor of One Federal Street (the views of Boston Harbor from the Regatta Room are stunning).

The Harvard Club was founded in 1908 by a group of twenty-two men who proposed the formation of a club exclusively for Harvard alumni. Dues were set at five dollars annually, and within a year the club had enlarged its membership rolls to 1,200 Harvard men—historically, private clubs were exclusively men only. By the 1940s women were relegated to a special annex. It wasn't until 1971, when Harvard became coed, that the Harvard Club voted to accept women as full members.

Harvard Hall, with its tapestries representing Harvard's undergraduate residential houses, represents pride of place for many club members. Resembling the Old-World style of a European Manor, Harvard

Hall is a stately space; the fireplaces are big enough to stand in, the silver chandeliers sparkle, the twenty-five-foot tall oak paneling gleams. "It is one of the most beautiful spaces in Boston that no one knows about," says Galvin. Karen Van Winkle, the current and first female president of the Harvard Club, adds, "People say it feels very Hogwarts in here."

Wander upstairs to the Massachusetts Room with its floor-to-ceiling windows that open out onto a balcony. This space is dedicated to Harvard alumni who have served in public office. The numbers are legion and include John Adams, Justice Stephen Breyer, and current Massachusetts Governor Charlie Baker.

Who's in and who's out? Full members need to have an affiliation to Harvard or be a graduate of Yale, MIT, or the Fletcher School of Law and Diplomacy at Tufts University. Membership is also available to faculty of both Harvard and MIT. Says Galvin, "Harvard and MIT have a long history of collaborating and many of our members have a degree from both." Those who do not meet this criteria may join the Harvard Club as associate members, with fewer privileges than full members.

Steep membership discounts are offered to young alumni. "I do think that younger people who are used to connecting through technology are looking for that face-to-face interaction. From a networking perspective, the Harvard Club is a phenomenal resource," says Van Winkle.

Being invited by a member for a long lunch or for after-work drinks is a time-honored way for the public to experience the Harvard Club. Members also often bring guests to the club's many life-long-learning events such as its Book Discussion Groups and Faculty Lecture Series. "Often our events have a lecture and cocktail component. It's social and intellectual and I think that is the sweet spot for much of what we do," Galvin explains.

Today's Harvard Club culture and policies are more relaxed, in keeping with contemporary lifestyles. The dress code for most places in the clubhouse is business casual, and members can also use technology anywhere in the club. Van Winkle says "Wearing a tie, or not allowing children into the club dining room; those days are gone."

JAPANESE GARDEN AT THE MFA

A POCKET OF TRANQUILITY

Boston's venerable and beloved Museum of Fine Arts is home to nearly five hundred thousand artworks from the far reaches of the globe. This is an art museum that really has it all—mummies; French Impressionists; a treasure trove of early-American art, including Paul Revere's famous Sons of Liberty silver bowl; and entire galleries dedicated to the works by John Singleton Copley, Gilbert Stuart, and John Singer Sargent.

But sometimes a little contemplation away from the exhibits is needed. One of the city's best-kept secret gardens is the MFA's *Tenshin-en*, the "Garden of the Heart of Heaven." Tucked next to the museum's west wing, the garden was created in 1988 out of the belief in the power of cultural exchange. The MFA has one of the largest collections of Japanese art outside of Japan. The garden honors the legacy of Okakura Kakuzo, one of the museum's first curators of Asian Art.

Tenshin-en is a captivating place, both inspiring and intimate. Walk through the traditional cypress gate and leave the world behind. Four unassuming masonry walls enclose the small—just ten thousand square feet—space. Inspired by the Zen temple gardens of fifteenth-century Japan, the garden's design is in the *karesansui*, or dry landscape style. The garden represents a miniature abstraction of nature, incorporating a

number of elements. Large rocks are placed singularly and in groups to represent mountains and islands. Raked gravel evokes the ripple of water. The overall garden design was also influenced by the landscape of the New England coast.

Some seventy species of plants—both Japanese and American—re-create the beauty of the New England hills and forest. Spring brings a show of flowers with cherry blossoms, azaleas, and iris. As spring turns to summer, the garden transitions to a more subdued color palette of soothing shades of green from conifers and ferns that rely on textural differences to create interest. Autumn is perhaps the most breathtaking time of the year to visit. For a few weeks each October, the garden's Japanese maples turn to fiery shades of crimson and gold.

A small, winding path creates mystery, and benches invite visitors to view the garden slowly and mindfully in all its detail. The garden is open to the public April through October during museum hours. Admission is always free—you don't need to buy a ticket to the MFA to visit.

KENDALL SQUARE ROOFTOP GARDEN

HEAD TO THE ROOF

Just across the Charles River in Cambridge, and a stone's throw from MIT, Kendall Square is the epicenter of tech start-ups in New England.

A flourishing rooftop garden is located at the sixth floor of the Kendall Center's Green Parking Garage. The garden is a haven of greenery and provides a respite to the academics and scientists who come to chill out on their lunch breaks.

Garden sanctuaries are, by nature, a little difficult to find. To access this rooftop garden, walk through the building's sleek first floor food court, go past the front desk, and take the elevator to the sixth floor.

The rooftop is home to a wonderful collection of colorful blooms, shade trees, a manicured lawn, vegetable gardens, and even a bee hive. There are paved walkways that lead to picnic tables and groupings of strategically placed, modernist Adirondack chairs. There's a Ping-Pong table too. And since the entire Kendall Square neighborhood has free and open high-speed Wi-Fi, there really is little reason to leave.

During the growing season (April through November), aspiring urban farmers can help with the planting and harvesting at the weekly Wednesday noon workshops run by Green City Growers. Jessie Babhazi, Green City Growers founder says, "We are at the garden the same time every week so that people who work in the building or in the area can come and engage and learn how to grow their own food and then all the produce is donated to community organizations."

MAPPARIUM

A WALK-IN GLOBE THAT'S
FROZEN IN TIME

For lovers of history and travel, a visit to the Mapparium, hidden within the headquarters of the Christian Science Church in Boston's Back Bay, may spark immediate wanderlust.

The luminous three-story walk-in globe depicts the oceans and continents, topography and countries. Visitors walk across a suspended glass bridge inside the globe for a unique look at the world—in its correct proportions and all at once.

The development of Boston's Back Bay, carved out of tidal flats in the late 1870s, symbolized the city's optimism and the prosperity that followed the Civil War. In the first decade of the twentieth century, a number of Boston cultural institutions—including the Boston Symphony and the Museum of Fine Arts—settled here. Among the first to call this neighborhood home was the original Mother Church of the First Church of Christ, Scientist, which was built in 1894 near the corner of Huntington and Massachusetts Avenues.

Along with the massive sanctuary of the expanded Mother Church, today's fourteen-acre church campus features an I.M. Pei–designed plaza that is the city's largest privately owned green space set aside for public use. The Mary Baker Eddy Library, named for the church's founder, houses the church's historic archives, its publishing house (which prints and distributes the church's magazines along with its Pulitzer prize–winning international newspaper, *The Christian Science Monitor*), and the Mapparium.

The Mapparium was conceived in the 1930s by Harvard-trained architect Chester Lindsay Churchill as the centerpiece of what was then the new Christian Science Publishing House.

The Mapparium was inspired by the gigantic revolving globe inside the lobby of the *New York Daily News* in Manhattan and was designed to represent the church's global outreach. Churchill envisioned the Mapparium as a space for people to come together, a place to experience a shared humanity and shared perspective of the world.

Made of 608 individual panels of hand-painted stained glass held together by a circular bronze framework—the Mapparium is a marvel of both engineering and cartography. Its scale approximates twenty-two miles to the inch and the metal bars accurately represent latitude and longitude at ten-degree intervals.

The Mapparium's kaleidoscope of color is coded to reflect the geographical and

political features of the world as it was in the 1930s. Churchill designed the Mapparium so that panels could be taken out and updated when countries changed their names and/or borders. Even as World War II forever altered geopolitical boundaries, it was decided that the Mapparium was a historic piece of art and architecture, and that it would forever represent the year of its completion.

Of course, the world today looks very different from the one depicted when the doors of the Mapparium first opened in 1935. In the Mapparium, Korea is ruled by Japan and is called Chosen. Israel was not established until 1948 and appears on the map as Palestine, while the name Iran was so new that Persia is also included in parentheses.

Bert Hogan, Assistant Manager of Visitor Services at the Mapparium, says, "The old saying that the sun never sets on the British Empire is still true in the Mapparium." The predominant color here is vivid red—much of it representing the United Kingdom and its territories. In the 1930s the British still governed India and large parts of Africa, while Canada and Australia were founding member states of the British Commonwealth of Nations.

Hogan also likes to point out the Aral Sea in the Soviet Union—what is now Russia. Once the fourth largest fresh water lake in the world, it has been entirely used up for irrigation and no longer exists on modern maps.

Another fun feature of the Mapparium is its unusual acoustics. Speak standing at the mid-point of the bridge and hear yourself in surround sound (because the glass doesn't absorb sound, it bounces off the walls in all directions). The Mapparium also has a whispering gallery effect. Send your companion across the bridge while you stand at one end. When you whisper, your companion will hear your voice as clearly as if you were standing next to them.

Tours of the Mapparium include both a docent-led introduction and a short sound and light show that illustrates how geography has changed over time. Churchill probably never imagined that eleven million people would cross the Mapparium's glass bridge. To walk inside the Mapparium today is to share the sense of wonder that this unique globe has evoked among people for generations.

METROPOLITAN
WATERWORKS MUSEUM

STEAM-POWERED WATER PUMPS:
A RELIC OF THE INDUSTRIAL AGE

Stand in the engine room of the Waterworks Museum, surrounded by the building's awe-inspiring architecture and you are immediately transported to the nineteenth century. At the heart of the complex is an impressive collection of three historic steam-powered water pumps. The site was decommissioned in the 1970s, but in its heyday, in the early 1900s, the steady throb of these engines pushed as much as a hundred million gallons of water a day to be delivered to taps throughout Boston and surrounding towns.

Today, we take easy access to reliable, safe drinking water for granted. But it hasn't always been that way. The lack of safe drinking water plagued Boston's early settlers. When the Puritan English colonists landed on the Shawmut Peninsula in 1630, the settlement's water supply essentially came from one spring.

Boston's modern water system dates from 1848 when water flowed down from a reservoir eight miles away in the town of Natick. It replaced a local patchwork of wells and pond water that was inadequate for the growing city, which resulted in water shortages and the outbreak of cholera and typhoid. It was said that 100,000 people gathered in Boston to celebrate the arrival of the new water system—significant as

the population of the city at the time would have been around twenty-five thousand people. Bands played and Boston's Frog Pond fountain shot a plume of water eighty feet in the air.

In the years immediately following the Civil War, manufacturing in the Boston area was booming and waves of immigrants—Irish, Italian, Russian Jews, and Canadians—led to overcrowding. A water infrastructure was deemed to be absolutely critical to the growth of the city.

Built in 1887 along the city's western edge where Boston converges with the town of Brookline and the city of Newton, the Waterworks Complex is a masterpiece of integrated design and was always intended to fit in with the landscape. A magnificent engine house, located on the banks of the Chestnut Hill Reservoir, disguised the furiously working machinery inside.

The Richardsonian Romanesque building was the site of the Chestnut Hill High Service Pumping Station. The engine room's

architect was Arthur H. Vinal and his design was greatly influenced by the sturdy, striking style of Henry Hobson Richardson (the renowned architect of Boston's Trinity Church). The massive building featured two types of local stone (grey granite and red sandstone), a cavernous entrance arch, multiple gables, and a turret. "This was the flagship station of the Boston water system. There is permanence to the architecture. You knew this was a building of importance," said Eric Peterson, the museum's Director of Operations.

Early on, Boston's water supply was backed by science. In 1889 the Boston Water Works hired George Whipple, a recent civil engineering graduate of MIT, to be director of the Chestnut Hill Laboratory. Whipple worked in relative obscurity in a small house on the hill behind the Water Works with a focus on biological water analyses. His book, *The Microscopy of Drinking Water*, is considered a seminal work in the field of sanitary engineering. Whipple eventually went on to help establish Harvard's School of Public Health.

The museum's earliest steam-powered water pump was designed by Erasmus Darwin Leavitt and was put into operation in 1894. It is nearly three stories tall and it's a beauty. Peterson points out the engine's brass and walnut detailing and its ship's wheel—a Leavitt trademark. "It wasn't just a machine. It had to have a flair and statement to it."

But just five years later, the city's water system was becoming overwhelmed again. In 1898 an engine from Milwaukee–based Allis-Chalmers was installed. The Allis engine proved to be a real workhorse—operating at the site until the middle of the twentieth century. The Allis engine is sixty-five feet tall with a marine motif and a spiral staircase. If the Allis engine's triple expansion design looks familiar, it's because it is almost exactly the same design as the steam engine on the *Titanic*.

The Worthington-Snow engine dates from 1922 and is the smallest of the engines in the exhibit. At the time, it was the highest, most refined engine that could be bought for the least amount of money. Soon after, the steam age was replaced by electric, diesel, and other forms of power. "Everybody moves on. You stand here and look at this equipment and you see the shift in industrial design and the end of an era," says Peterson.

Visitors can tour the Waterworks Museum on their own, but know that Waterworks volunteers are a passionate lot and really enjoy explaining the marvel of how these engines worked. Let them.

MOUNT AUBURN CEMETERY

ART AND HISTORY AMONG BOSTON'S DEAD

It may not be a visitor's first pick of a Boston park, but Mount Auburn Cemetery, located on 170 acres of mature woodland on the border of Cambridge and Watertown, offers a fascinating walk for visitors interested in Boston history, art, and natural beauty.

It is a place of ornate tombs and haunting mausoleums, as well as majestic trees, winding paths, picturesque vistas, and birdsong. It is a deeply emotional place.

Many come to pay their respects to notables as varied as writers Henry Wadsworth Longfellow and Bernard Malamud, abolitionist Charles Sumner, philanthropist Isabella Stewart Gardner, painter Winslow Homer, inventor and cofounder of the Polaroid Corporation Edwin Land, and sports broadcaster Curt Gowdy.

The establishment of Mount Auburn Cemetery in 1831 marked the birth of the rural cemetery movement in the United States. Mount Auburn was created as the city's first large burial ground in part because of growing concerns about the overcrowding of cemeteries and the spread of disease. Up until that time the dead were buried in church yards, the town commons, or in small family plots.

Mount Auburn's very beginnings are rooted in horticulture—the cemetery was one of the first collaborative landscape designs in the country. Mount Auburn's was created as a pastoral haven by a group of well-connected Bostonians, including Dr. Jacob Bigelow, a physician and Harvard professor of botany; and Henry A. S. Dearborn, one

of the founders of the Massachusetts Horticultural Society.

Meg Winslow, Mount Auburn's curator of historical collections, says that the sale of cemetery lots was also going to fund an experimental garden, "as a way to introduce new kinds of plants, fruits, and vegetables to New Englanders."

Winslow points out that in the early nineteenth century Boston had no Museum of Fine Arts, there was no Museum of Science, and there were few public parks. "When visitors came to Boston, they always came to Mount Auburn Cemetery. They climbed Washington Tower and looked out from the land of the dead to the land of living 125 feet above the Charles River."

Among Mount Auburn's many historically significant works of art is its elaborate granite entrance gate in the Egyptian Revival style suggesting the triumphal passage from the mundane world to the next. Bigelow commissioned the cemetery's 1845 Great Rose Window for the chapel, an important early example of stained glass in America. And, of late, there is a lot of interest in the 1872 marble statue of *Hygeia*, the goddess of health, commissioned by Dr. Harriot Kezia Hunt, one of the first female physicians in Boston, for her family's lot. Hunt chose Edmonia Lewis, a sculptress of African-American and Chippewa ancestry to create

the piece. Both Hunt and Lewis were pioneers in their fields and the symbolism of Hygeia, a woman as a possessor of power, is not lost on those who visit Hunt's grave.

Today Mount Auburn's plant collections are still exceptional with meticulously maintained gardens and nearly 5,000 cataloged trees. Mount Auburn is also the first American cemetery to be accredited as an arboretum with significant stands of red oak, sugar maple, and flowering dogwood.

All those flowers and trees create a sanctuary for birds—and Mount Auburn is known throughout the world as a birding hotspot. According to Winslow, "The citizen science effort at Mount Auburn is extraordinary. Bird walks are regularly scheduled and are among Mount Auburn's most popular events.

"Mount Auburn's landscape continually evolves," says Winslow. "It's not one

landscape that we preserve so that it always looks like that. We keep changing it. We keep working it. Initially Mount Auburn was designed to look natural. It was a natural landscape that looked like no hand had shaped it. But it has been shaped and it continues to be shaped today."

As a tourist destination, Mount Auburn offers great access to visitors. Sinslow says, "Today we really want people to know that they are welcome. We are open to the public 365 days of the year, dawn to dusk and free of charge."

The busiest day of the year at Mount Auburn is Mother's Day, but the cemetery's various dog monuments are the most beloved (although dogs are not buried here). Be advised, though, that Mount Auburn is an active cemetery, so there is an aspect of "no access" when there is a funeral or memorial service taking place. Despite a steady influx of visitors—some 250,000 people visit annually—Mount Auburn remains both a sacred space as well as a tranquil and beautiful oasis.

N.C. WYETH MURALS AT THE LANGHAM HOTEL BOSTON

ART, HISTORY, AND COMMERCE

The Langham Boston is one of the more unexpected places in the city to see fine art. Walk through the hotel's lobby and up a small set of stairs to a second-floor function room with rich paneled walls, a gold-painted coffered ceiling, and expansive floor-to-ceiling windows. Together, it makes a fitting backdrop for two 1920s murals by N.C. Wyeth that chronicle America's banking history.

The Langham Hotel takes over most of a city block in Boston's Financial District and occupies the 1922 building that was once Boston's Federal Reserve Bank. The fortress-like office building was designed in a Neo-Renaissance style with a long façade, great bronze doors, and a painted domed ceiling. Eventually, The Federal Reserve outgrew the space and in 1977 moved to nearby Atlantic Avenue.

The 1920s was considered the golden age of American Illustration, as there was a growing demand for artwork in magazines and books. At the time, N.C. Wyeth was one of America's preeminent illustrators, beloved for his drawings of classic children's adventure stories such as Robert Louis Stevenson's *Treasure Island*. But Wyeth was also well known for his work as a muralist. And while he and his family (notably his son, painter Andrew Wyeth) are mostly associated with Chadds Ford, Pennsylvania, Wyeth was, in fact, a displaced New Englander, having been born and raised in Needham,

Massachusetts. In fact, Wyeth's young family temporarily returned to Needham from 1921 to 1923 while he worked on the Federal Reserve murals.

The impressive paintings were commissioned to preside over the Governor's Reception rooms of the Boston Federal Reserve. Now called the Wyeth Room, it's not hard to imagine the city's business leaders and their bankers strengthening their relationship here over a glass of whiskey.

The room speaks for itself, says Debbie Freckleton, the Langham's Director of Quality, Learning and Development.

One wall depicts President George Washington, Revolutionary War financier Robert Morris, and First Secretary of the Treasury Alexander Hamilton. These days, Lin-Manuel Miranda's hit musical about "the ten-dollar Founding Father without a father" has suddenly made Hamilton very popular. It's hard to say how many people tramp through The Langham to seek out the murals, but this is one of the few Alexander Hamilton connections in the city.

On the opposite wall, Abraham Lincoln is shown with his Secretary of the Treasury, Salmon P. Chase. Freckleton often gives presentations to small groups interested in the building's history. She points out that Chase ran against Lincoln for the 1860 Republican presidential nomination, but was chosen by Lincoln to join his cabinet. Chase is considered to be one of the country's more notable Treasury heads—he was responsible for creating both the Bureau of Engraving and Printing and for establishing the Internal Revenue Service.

Wyeth's idealized and powerful images of Washington and Lincoln reinforced the patriotic and moral purpose of the banker's work. Wyeth's association with the treasury actually spanned decades. In the early 1940s he illustrated posters encouraging Americans to buy war bonds.

"These murals aren't going anywhere," says Freckleton. "We are fortunate that the hotel has been designated a landmark by the Boston Landmarks Commission and that the Federal Reserve did not take the Wyeth portraits with them when they moved."

Converted into a hotel in the early 1980s and part of the Langham Hotel Group since 2003, this is one of the city's most refined hotels. At the time of this writing, the hotel is closed and undergoing an extensive renovation. It is expected to reopen in 2020.

OLD NORTH CHURCH

BEHIND THE SCENES TOUR OF THE CHURCH THAT HELPED START A REVOLUTION

On Sunday morning the bells of Old North Church ring for an entire hour, their peals not so much a melody, but a river of sound that can be heard throughout the North End, Boston's Italian-American neighborhood.

Old North Church, also known as Christ Church, was built in 1723 and is Boston's oldest active church. The Reverend Stephen Ayres, the current vicar of the Episcopalian congregation says, "We are the custodians of two traditions at Old North, the church and the historic site. We are in the values business."

The eight bells at the top of the church's belfry are nearly as old—they date from 1744 and were forged in Gloucester, England. "They were the first ring of bells made by the British in North America and they are a treasure," says Ayres. Originally, local boys were tasked with ringing the bells. Among the signees of a 1750 church contract to pay ringers two cents a week—a fifteen-year-old Paul Revere.

The North End was Paul Revere's neighborhood. Revere's home, the oldest single-family structure in Boston, still stands—just around the corner on Salem Street. In Revere's time, Christ Church—with its 190-foot steeple—was the tallest building in Boston. Surely Revere knew the inner workings of the church when he made arrangements with Sexton Robert Newman to signal the colonists of British troop movement by lantern—"One if by land, two if by sea."

Old North Church is a stop on Boston's Freedom Trail, the two-and-a-half-mile path that wends its way past sixteen sites of the city's patriotic past. It is a good walk. By the time visitors reach Old North Church, most are content to file into the high-walled family box pews for an opportunity to rest—and dutifully listen to a church educator's five-minute spiel on the lantern story.

Poet Henry Wadsworth Longfellow's words, "Listen my child and you shall hear of the midnight ride of Paul Revere," immortalized what was until that time the obscure story of a Patriot silversmith, engraver, and some-time courier. The educators point out that Longfellow used quite a bit of poetic license with the historic facts relating to the events of April 18, 1775—and they are happy to set the record straight.

Revere did not ride alone, there were at least two other riders that evening. Also, the lantern signals were not for Revere, but rather from Revere. Finally, the twin lanterns were never hung in the church belfry—they were held aloft for just enough time to allow the Sons of Liberty in Charlestown to know that British troops would cross the Charles River by rowboat rather than march across Boston Neck on their way to Lexington and Concord.

The drop-in talk only scratches the surface of the church's remarkable history. To delve deeper, take a "Behind the Scenes" tour. These small-group, guided visits are scheduled each day and allow special access up into the bell tower and down into the crypt hidden deep beneath the church's floor.

A small, steep staircase leads to the tour's first stop—the church archive room. Historic drawings and photographs detail some of the church's architectural features. Old North's classical design—a red brick meeting house topped by a gleaming white wooden spire—was inspired by Christopher Wren, the architect behind London's St. Paul's Cathedral.

Old North has always been a dignified, contemplative house of worship. But early in its history, the church was at the center of some Colonial shenanigans. In 1757 a traveling aerialist decided to make a couple of pennies by gathering a crowd and telling one and all that he could jump off the tower of Christ Church. His trick? He slid down a guide wire that he ran from the top of the steeple along Hull Street to Copps Hill Burying Ground. The people loved it. The next week, there were huge crowds (so it is said) to see the stunt. Some folks did not go to work. By the third occasion of the jump, authorities arrested the aerialist on trumped up charges because he was affecting the local economy. In Colonial Boston, people worked six days a week.

Another narrow set of stairs brings visitors up to the bell ringing chamber. The bronze bells are tucked into the belfry two floors above and range in size from five hundred pounds (the highest pitch) to fifteen hundred pounds (the lowest pitch). These are change-ringing bells. The sound is created when ringers stand in a circle—one behind each rope—and pull the bells in different combinations. There are more than forty thousand possible patterns! Perhaps it is not at all surprising that the Massachusetts Institute of Technology Guild of Bellringers is the resident bell-ringing club.

The last tour stop is a walk through the maze of tunnels underneath the church. The squeamish will be glad to know that this is a historical/atmospheric burial chamber visit—there are not any bones or skulls on view. And while the wooden floors are creaky when visiting the sanctuary, the sound of tourists' feet is thunderous overhead when walking in the crypt.

The entrance to the crypt is behind a locked door that opens into a small room. This modern columbarium is tastefully designed with niches to hold cremated remains and regularly welcomes new inhabitants today.

One of the more notable tombs here is that of Samuel Nicholson, the first commander of the USS *Constitution*. A tour docent points out that the tomb is all fancied up because once each year they bring the new, young Navy cadets serving on Old Ironsides to pay their proper respects to Captain Nicholson.

In the 1700s it was the custom of the Anglican Church to have people buried in graveyards that were connected to the church. The Puritan leadership of Boston that existed at the time would not sell the church land to bury their dead, so the church built an underground crypt. Ultimately thirty-seven barrel-shaped tombs were created, with as many as eleven hundred bodies buried here. The crypt was used from 1732, but even from its inception, there was not enough room. At various times they swept out some of the old bones and put them in a communal charnel pit.

The charnel created fumes and was deemed a health hazard by the city. Eventually, the city came in and cemented everything over and from 1860 to 1991 there was not a burial of any kind at Old North Church.

PUPPET FREE LIBRARY

EXPLORE A WONDROUS REPOSITORY

Tucked in an alley behind Newbury Street's chic boutiques, a hand-written sign above a wooden hobbit doorway marks the entrance to Boston's Puppet Free Library.

Pull the iron bell for entrance. When we did, Sara Peattie, a diminutive woman wearing a paint-splattered apron, opened the door. "Are you here to see the puppets?" she asked cheerfully. But of course!

Duck inside and head through what feels like a parallel universe filled with all manner of fantastical characters—dancing stilt fairies, thirty-foot-long dragons, and a menagerie of hybrid animals created out of papier-mâché, cardboard, paint, and bits of cloth.

Part working art studio, part storage vault, and part puppet lending library, this is one of Boston's art scene's hidden gems. Peattie is a nationally acclaimed puppeteer and the co-founder of the Puppeteer's Cooperative, which has specialized in creating puppets for theater, as well as for community pageants, since 1976. But Peattie is most well-known for her giant puppets that have become a mainstay of First Night Boston, the city's New Year's Eve art and culture extravaganza.

Located in the basement of Emmanuel Church, this wondrous repository is not advertised. It's mostly word-of-mouth that brings the curious to seek out the puppets—and Peattie. Emmanuel is just a stroll from Boston's Public Garden. Designed in an

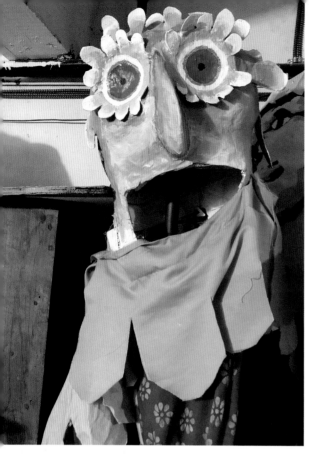

elaborate Gothic Revival style, the church dates from 1861 and was the first building constructed on Newbury Street. Emmanuel has a reputation as one of the city's most progressive and welcoming faith communities with a long history of ministry through the arts. "Puppeteers and puppets have been at Emmanuel since the 1960s. We get along very well," says Peattie.

Peattie's puppetry draws people together, even if just for a moment. Her latest project is a portable puppet theater that drops inside Emmanuel's entryway. The puppet shows engage both Newbury Street shoppers and wayward tourists. "It's a theater, but it's also an art installation," she explains.

"My inspiration is mostly nature. That's the great thing about puppetry, you are not reduced to this narrow, human world. You have the whole universe of animals, plants, and things like the sun and the moon. And you can create characters out of abstract concepts like justice and peace."

Peattie is one of Boston's citizen artists who give the city its inimitable character. On sunny weekends, she can sometimes be found across the street at the Boston Public Garden dressed as her alter ego, Ms. Mouse. Wearing a giant friendly mouse mask and a granny dress and shawl, Peattie

sits knitting on a park bench next to a cart filled with masks, colorful streamers, and a sign that reads, "Take what you like, give what you want." Kids and grownups can play with the props and make their own joyous puppet mayhem in the park. Says Peattie, "It's a way to share art for all."

On Tuesday afternoons (or by appointment) visitors to Peattie's basement studio are welcome to learn about the ancient art of puppetry. Peattie will even let visitors take the puppets out to play—for a few hours or a few weeks—with just a signature and phone number—no strings attached.

THE SACRED COD

BOSTON'S MOST STORIED FISH

A painted wooden fish hangs high above the Massachusetts House of Representatives. Made of solid pine, the nearly five-foot replica cod weighs in at eighty pounds. The Sacred Cod, as it is known, is the third to preside over the Massachusetts legislature, and was a gift to Massachusetts lawmakers in 1784 by merchant Jonathan Rowe (Boston's Rowes Wharf is named for him).

"It was said that when the colonists first settled in Boston that there was so much cod in the waters of Massachusetts that the fishermen could just reach out and put their hands out in the water to catch them."

Mary Rinehart, Director of Massachusetts State House Tours, certainly is enthusiastic describing the importance of the fishing industry to the commonwealth. "The Sacred Cod is a very special symbol and the number-one topic asked of our guides," she says.

The Sacred Cod originally hung in the Old State House on Washington Street. The current State House, located on Beacon Hill, was designed by Charles Bulfinch, considered one of the leading architects of Colonial America. With its gold dome, it is one of the city's most prominent landmarks. Bulfinch's Federalist design became a model for many state capital buildings. When completed in 1798, the cod was wrapped

in an American flag and brought to the State House in a grand procession.

The Sacred Cod has always been in the State House except for a brief time in 1933 when it was brazenly cod-napped by staff of the *Harvard Lampoon,* the university's monthly humor magazine. "There was a great outrage by members of the House and they refused to have any sessions. It soon became clear that the theft was a college prank and the Sacred Cod was returned after just a few days," says Rinehart.

There was another codnapping attempt in the 1960s, says Rinehart. "The Sacred Cod has now been hung much higher and out of harm's way."

The Sacred Cod can best be viewed from the fourth-floor public gallery or from the floor of the House Chamber when taking a free State House tour (offered Monday through Friday, call in advance to reserve).

SALADA TEA DOORS

TELLING THE STORY OF TEA IN BRONZE

If it wasn't for the plaque on the outside of the building, visitors would never guess that this was once the world headquarters for Salada Tea, a Montreal company founded in 1892 by Peter Larkin. The company was a pioneer in the tea industry—and among the first to package tea in foil that sealed out air and moisture. At the time, foil-wrapped tea bags was a game changer and by 1917, Larkin moved Salada's factory headquarters to Boston's Park Square.

The otherwise plain façade of this rather non-descript ten-story office building features a set of spectacular bronze doors designed by English sculptor Henry Wilson in 1927. Wilson was one of the leading artists of the Arts and Crafts movement, and today is most known for creating the west door of the Cathedral of St. John the Divine in New York City.

The twelve-foot, two-ton doors show a sequence of ten intricate bas-relief panels. They depict scenes of the late-nineteenth-century tea trade in Ceylon (now Sri Lanka) from harvest to drying to the loading of tea crates on clipper ships. The doors are further embellished with figures of South East Asian deities and elephants—exotic themes for American art at the time. But perhaps most shocking of all are the many figures of well-muscled tea workers in loin cloths. By the 1920s, the city's notorious literary

censor, the Watch and Ward Society, was at the height of its power making "banned in Boston" a national catch-phrase. The doors smacked of impropriety in the respectable social circles of old Yankee money.

The marble outer door frame, sculpted by Wilson's assistant, M. Caesar Caira, is classically inspired and deserves a closer look as well. Just under the roofline is Demeter, the Greek goddess of grain and the harvest along with a frieze of elephants. The doors are also flanked by pilasters—each is adorned with a female Greek goddess and capped with still more elephant carvings.

For the tea executives who would pass through this grand passageway, the doors represented a strong visual narrative of Salada's company culture and were a powerful reminder of the firm's prosperity.

Salada left Boston in the 1950s after being acquired by a multinational food company. Still known locally as the Salada Tea building, the office tower has been owned by Liberty Mutual Insurance since

2004. Says the company's Communications Spokesperson Adrianne Kaufmann, "Liberty Mutual's plans are to keep the doors as they are and maintain them in place for public enjoyment."

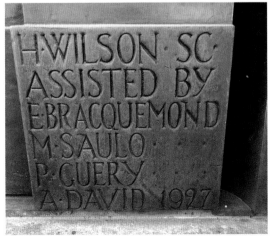

SKINNY HOUSE

A CASE OF SIBLING RIVALRY
GONE TOO FAR

Boston's North End is home not only to the narrowest streets, but also the narrowest of houses. Sandwiched between two large brick buildings and directly on the Freedom Trail, the townhouse dubbed the "Skinny House" is a modern tourist attraction in its own right.

Built in the 1880s, the four-story home is located across the street from Copps Hill Burying Ground. Dating from 1659, this is the second-oldest cemetery in the city and is the resting place of firebrand preacher Cotton Mather. Musket ball pock marks on some gravestones are said to be evidence that British troops used the burying ground for target practice.

The Skinny House is referred to as a spite house because it was built with the specific purpose to annoy. According to local legend, two brothers inherited this plot of land from their father. When one brother was away fighting the Civil War, the other brother built a large home on their shared lot, leaving just a sliver of land for his brother. Denied his inheritance, the returning soldier built the Skinny House to block out the light and the view of his brother's house.

Today, the Skinny House is a two-bedroom family home, but that doesn't stop hordes of visitors from standing across the street on the steps leading to the Copps Hill entrance gate to take photos. Measuring in at ten feet and four inches at its widest point, this is the narrowest house in Boston. Note that the "front" door is on the side of the house in the alley. Inside the house, at its narrowest, a tape measure would only stretch to six feet and two inches—close enough to touch the two side walls at once.

UNDERGROUND AT INK BLOCK

A HIGHWAY UNDERPASS PARK
THAT IS FUNCTIONAL AND BEAUTIFUL

Ink Block is the place to be in Boston. In the shadow of what was the old headquarters of the *Boston Herald*, a wave of new development has transformed the once run-down northeastern section of Boston's South End neighborhood with up-scale condos, retail, and restaurants.

Part of the bid to develop the parcel included a program to develop underutilized city space. Alongside a new parking lot, Underground at Ink Block is a seven-acre public park located underneath the I-93 overpass.

"We wanted to make sure that the park was a great amenity for the entire neighborhood. Most importantly it links South Boston and the South End," says Kathy McMahon, a vice-president at National Development, the operator of the park.

But Underground at Ink Block is not just about getting from point A to point B. It's a scenic spot to hang out. The bike paths and pedestrian boardwalk along the Fort Point Channel are a huge draw for both residents and visitors. The underpass itself is greatly enlivened by its 150,000 square feet of mural walls. Says McMahon, "The murals have been a huge hit. People come down all the time to take photos. Several couples have been engaged in front of our love mural."

The park also regularly sponsors events like movie nights, parties with live music and food trucks, and free yoga classes. Opened in the fall of 2017, this once-forgotten area has become a new community gathering space.

WINTER STREET CONCOURSE

THE T'S HANDY HIDDEN
PEDESTRIAN TUNNEL

The legacy of Boston's T runs as deep as the subterranean tracks themselves. Inaugurated on September 1, 1897, Boston's T is the country's first subway. Known as the "T," short for the Massachusetts Bay Transportation Authority, it is the municipal service that Bostonians love to hate. We gripe and complain about the T's service delays, crowded trolleys, and frequent fare hikes, but most Bostonians rely on the T every day for commuting and have a powerful connection to their neighborhood station—it's part of what they associate with home.

Navigating the T is a challenge for even native Bostonians. Many commuters don't know that T riders can use a pedestrian tunnel at Park Street station to walk to the Downtown Crossing station and transfer from the Green to the Orange line without taking a train. It's quicker to walk between the stations, it's useful in inclement weather, and you can avoid the gauntlet of people on Washington Street handing out flyers.

Massachusetts Department of Transportation spokesperson Lisa Battiston says the Winter Street Concourse currently exists within the fare gates of each station, so

customers who have tapped a CharlieCard or used a CharlieTicket to gain entry to either station have access to the concourse.

Follow the Winter Street Concourse signs from either the Green Line at Park Street or the Orange Line at Downtown Crossing. Not sure if you are headed in the right direction underground? The T uses color coding to keep riders on track. When walking toward Park Street Station, the concourse columns are painted green, when walking toward Downton Crossing, the columns are painted orange.

Bostonians call the subway lines by their colors. Since the 1960s the four main branches of the T have been color-coded to be easier to identify and navigate. The T's colors aren't random—like nearly everything in Boston, each color has a historical reference. The Green Line winds through the heart of the city and Frederick Law Olmsted's Emerald Necklace park system. The Red Line goes out to Cambridge, home of Harvard University—crimson red is Harvard's official color. The origin of the Blue Line is easy to guess—as its route runs along Boston Harbor. The Orange Line's moniker is trickier—its name dates back to the city's earliest days when this part of present-day Washington Street was named Orange Street.

APPENDIX

All Saints Way
4 Battery St.
Boston, MA 02109

Bear Cage Hill
Franklin Park
Boston, MA 02121
(617) 635-4505
boston.gov

Black Heritage Trail
(617) 742-5415
nps.gov/boaf/planyourvisit/hours.htm

Bodega
6 Clearway St.
Boston, MA 02115
shop.bdgastore.com

The Boston Athenaeum
10½ Beacon St.
Boston, MA 02108
(617) 227-0270
bostonathenaeum.org

Boston Harbor Islands
Long Wharf North Ticket Center
66 Long Wharf
Boston, MA
(617) 223-8666
bostonharborislands.org

Boston Harbor Islands Welcome Center
Corner of State Street and Atlantic Avenue
Boston, MA 02109
(617) 223-8666
bostonharborislands.org/bostonlight

Boston Public Library
Courtyard Restaurant
700 Boylston St.
Boston, MA 02116
(617) 859-2251
thecateredaffair.com

Boston Symphony Hall
301 Massachusetts Ave.
Boston, MA 02115
(617) 266-1492
bso.org

Brattle Book Shop

9 West St.

Boston, MA 02111

(617) 542-0210

brattlebookshop.com

Brook Farm Historic Site

670 Baker St.

West Roxbury, MA 02132

Central Burying Ground

Boston Common

Boylston and Tremont Sreets

Boston, MA 02116

(617) 635-7361

boston.gov/cemeteries/
central-burying-ground

Custom House Tower

Marriott Vacation Club Pulse

3 McKinley Sq.

Boston, MA 02109

(617) 310-6300

marriott.com/hotels/travel/bosch-marriott-
vacation-club-pulse-at-custom-house-
boston/

Ether Dome

Massachusetts General Hospital

55 Fruit St.

Boston, MA 02114

(617) 726-2000

massgeneral.org

Exchange Place Staircase

53 State St.

Boston, MA

statestreet.com

Fenway Farms

4 Jersey St.

Boston, MA 02215

greencitygrowers.com

Fenway Victory Gardens

1200 Boylston St.

Boston, MA 02215

(857) 244-0262

fenwayvictorygardens.org

Harvard Art Museums

32 Quincy St.

Cambridge, MA 02138

(617) 495-9400

harvardartmuseums.org

The Harvard Club of Boston

374 Commonwealth Ave.

Boston, MA 02215

(617) 536-1260

Japanese Garden

Museum of Fine Arts

465 Huntington Ave.

Boston, MA 02115

(617) 267-9300

mfa.org

Kendall Square Rooftop Garden

Kendall Center's Green Parking Garage

90 Broadway St.

Cambridge, MA 02142

(617) 252-7140

kendallcenter.com

The Lanham, Boston

250 Franklin St.

Boston, MA

(617) 451-1900

langhamhotels.com/en/the-langham/
boston

The Mapparium

Mary Baker Eddy Library

200 Massachusetts Ave.

Boston, MA 02115

(617) 450-7000

marybakereddylibrary.org

Massachusetts State House

24 Beacon St.

Boston, MA 02133

(617) 727-3676

malegislature.gov

Metropolitan Waterworks Museum

2450 Beacon St.

Boston MA 02467

(617) 277-0065

waterworksmuseum.org

Mount Auburn Cemetery

580 Mount Auburn St.

Cambridge, MA 02138

(617) 547-7105

mountauburn.org

Old North Church

193 Salem St.

Boston, MA 02113

(617) 858-8231

oldnorth.com

Puppet Free Library

15 Public Alley #437

Boston, MA 02116

(617) 536-3355

puppetco-op.org

Salada Tea Headquarters

330 Stuart St.

Boston, MA 02116

The Skinny House

44 Hull St.

Boston, MA 02113

Underground at Ink Block

Intersection of Traveler and Albany Streets

Boston, MA 02118

undergroundinkblock.com

Winter Street Concourse

Park Street Station and

Downtown Crossing Station

Boston, MA

(617) 222-3200

mbta.com

INDEX

PHOTO CREDITS

ACKNOWLEDGMENTS

Writing *No Access Boston* would not have been possible without the support of my family. With appreciation to my dad and mom, Bob and Jo Dascanio. I was fortunate to grow up with parents who loved to travel. Special thanks to my husband, Masoud, for supporting me as I pursued my dream job of being a travel writer. Thank you to my sons Bijan, Kian, and Camy for their unending patience and encouragement. Finally, with gratitude to my daughter Leda for her amazing photography skills—this book is better for it! Many thanks and much love to all.

ABOUT THE AUTHOR

MARIA OLIA is a travel writer and essay-ist. Her writing has appeared in the *Boston Globe* and *Working Mother* as well as many other national publications. She has written six Boston/New England travel books, including *Day Trips New England, Discovering Vintage Boston,* and *New England's Colonial Inns and Taverns: Centuries of Yankee Fare and Hospitality,* all for Globe Pequot Press.

A near-native New Englander, Maria has called Massachusetts her home for almost four decades. She is endlessly curious about Boston's culture and history and enjoys discovering new places as much as she does celebrating old favorites.

She lives just a short trolley ride from Boston—in the neighboring town of Newton with her husband, and delights in the occasional visits from her four grown children.

Catch up with Maria on her website mariaolia.com.